SWATT
ARCHITECTS

SWATT ARCHITECTS

LIVABLE MODERN

FOREWORD BY RAY KAPPE
INTRODUCTION BY CORY BUCKNER

First published in Australia in 2004 by
The Images Publishing Group Pty Ltd
ABN 89 059 734 431
6 Bastow Place, Mulgrave, Victoria, 3170, Australia
Telephone: +61 3 9561 5544 Facsimile: +61 3 9561 4860
books@images.com.au
www.imagespublishinggroup.com

Copyright © The Images Publishing Group Pty Ltd
The Images Publishing Group Reference Number: 359

All rights reserved. Apart from any fair dealing for the purposes of private study,
research, criticism, or review as permitted under the Copyright Act, no part of
this publication may be reproduced, stored in a retrieval system, or transmitted
in any form by any means, electronic, mechanical, photocopying, recording,
or otherwise, without the written permission of the publisher.

National Library of Australia Cataloguing-in-Publication data
Swatt Architects: livable modern

Includes index.
ISBN 1 920744 45 2

1. Architecture, Domestic—California—Pictorial works.
I. Swatt Architects.

728.09794

Designed by The Graphic Image Studio Pty Ltd, Australia
www.tgis.com.au

Film by Mission Productions Limited, Hong Kong
Printed by Everbest Printing Co. Ltd. in Hong Kong/China

IMAGES has included on its website a page for special notices in relation to this
and its other publications. Please visit: www.imagespublishinggroup.com

Contents

Foreword
Ray Kappe

Almost 40 years ago a young aspiring architecture student came to my office. He had just completed his first year at the University of California, Berkeley, and he shared his design projects with me. We discussed each of them. One was a tetrahedral structure that he did not consider to be architecture. I said that I thought it was architecture since it was an intelligent structure that enclosed space. From there we continued to discuss architecture and architects. I was impressed with him and thought that he would probably evolve into a successful architect someday. As we spoke, he became somewhat disturbed that he did not have greater knowledge of more architects and their contributions. I later learned that after our conversation he considered giving up architecture. Fortunately he reconsidered.

Robert Swatt continued to stay in touch with me in the years that followed. He graduated from Berkeley and did his apprenticeship with Howard Friedman, a friend of mine in San Francisco (who, interestingly, had been a mentor to me when I was a student), and later with Cesar Pelli in Los Angeles.

Upon starting his own practice, like many young artists and architects he explored architectural design by referring to the work of other architects. In the Friedman office he designed a house which referenced my own house, but in his own office the earliest work was simple, clean modern architecture, probably influenced by another mentor, Don Olsen, one of his professors at Berkeley. There was then a period of work with historical references to architects such as Irving Gill and Rudolph Schindler. This was architecture that he was familiar with prior to his architectural education. Other work was connected to the architecture of the Bay Area, and finally there was a residence in which he worked with unusual shapes and form. Many of these projects won design awards, but for Robert they represented an exploration and were part of his personal evolution.

During the late 1970s and all through the 1980s, the advocates of the post-modern movement were questioning modern architecture. Retrogressive historicism and new formalism replaced the tenets of modern architecture which had been clear in the preceding decades and followed by most of my generation. It was difficult for young offices to establish a singular design direction due to these numerous influences. It was fortunate for Swatt that during most of this period his major client was Levi Strauss & Co. He was designing new factories for them in the USA and Europe. These were projects that were not influenced by the philosophical debate between modern and post-modern.

In his residential work, he was influenced enough by the prevailing design discourse to search out the historical roots of early California modern architecture through Gill and Schindler, as I stated before, and also try his hand at the new formalism. But he did not truly leave his belief in modern architecture.

By 1990, there was a visible maturation in Robert Swatt's architecture beginning with The Icehouse, which was a masterful insertion within two existing buildings. His major residential breakthrough was the house he designed for himself and his family in 1995. This was a piece of architecture that spoke in his own words. It was a composition of several elements brought together in a pleasing composition. It encompassed the beautiful site, framing exceptional views and creating within the structure wonderful spaces. The progression from the carport to the entry door, the view upon entering over the living-dining space to the trees and hills beyond, and the movement along the skylit gallery with stairs leading down to the living-dining space in one direction, the view to an outside court in the other direction or to the stairway ahead to the second level are all beautifully orchestrated. The exposed structure throughout this portion of the house reinforces the horizontal extensions to the garden.

Robert Swatt's own residence communicated positively to many people, demonstrated by the quantity of work that followed. From this project, most of the work shown in this monograph became reality. Swatt continued to employ elements of his vocabulary to create a group of exceptional residences. Each expresses the uniqueness of the client but within an architecture that is recognizably Robert Swatt. It is not that the vocabulary is identical from project to project, but in each case it is an exploration built upon a set of principles that are evolving with mature control and a greater certainty.

Robert Swatt's architecture does not attempt to be 'cutting edge'. It does not distort space, have leaning walls, or an overabundance of materials and design fragments. It is based upon timeless principles of modern architecture. It is responsive to the client and site, uses proper shading devices, is environmentally sound, expresses structure when appropriate, uses open planning and diminishes the barrier between the interior and exterior. His work is simple and clear, usually orthogonal, but with excellent spatial qualities.

Robert Swatt is still a young architect, but he has reached a successful stage in his career which has a clarity that can only continue to evolve and become stronger in the future. I look forward to watching his evolution.

Above: Robert Swatt and Ray Kappe

Introduction

Cory Buckner

In *Art and Life in America*, art historian Oliver Larkin chose Frank Lloyd Wright's Falling Water, Gropius' house at Lincoln, Massachusetts, and Richard Neutra's Emerson Junior High School in Los Angeles (Fig.1)[1] as leading examples of 1930s modernism. It would be an interesting study to see how many former students of Emerson Junior High School have turned to architecture as their profession or primary interest in life. We know of one student, Robert Swatt, who remembers classrooms filled with natural light from the 15-foot-tall glass and steel sliding doors. These doors opened to outdoor classrooms drenched in sun. Such an early experience with remarkable architecture

is quite clearly one of the reasons why, at the early age of 13, a young Angelino turned his sights to the profession of architecture.

Years later, he discovered the work of the other great Southern California modernist architect, R.M. Schindler, whom Swatt's grandmother, Pauline Meyer Sternberger, had hired to design the Nobby Knit Shop in Los Angeles in 1930 (Fig. 2). The Nobby Knit Shop became a successful women's wear chain, the first in the Los Angeles area. Sternberger's creativity extended beyond her fine eye for architecture: she taught her young grandson to paint with oils at the young age of eight.

Further familial influence included Swatt's uncle, Joe Morris, who owned the art deco Shangri-La Hotel in Santa Monica. Morris hired Swatt when he was just out of university to design a remodel for the structure. It remains today one of the outstanding buildings along Ocean Avenue, a popular tourist area.

The University of California at Berkeley in the early 1960s was one of the leading architecture schools in the nation. In the past it had boasted successful alumni such as William Wilson Wurster, Ray Kappe, and John Funk. Swatt enrolled in 1965, a year after the Free Speech Movement. He studied with Don Olsen and William Turnbull. Turnbull and his contemporaries, including his partners Charles Moore and Donlyn Lyndon, were influenced by the work of Louis Kahn and Alvar Aalto. In a reaction against the International Style, they borrowed heavily from California wood sheathed outbuildings and barns to create a new Bay Area architectural tradition, with its own design language and philosophy.

At Berkeley, Swatt met, taught with, and later worked with Howard A. Friedman. Friedman taught Swatt to

Fig 1 Emerson Junior High School

1 See Thomas S. Hines, Richard Neutra and the Search for Modern Architecture, New York and Oxford: Oxford University Press, 1982, p.166

Fig 2 Nobby Knit Shop

value the social aspects of architecture, working for organizations like Dominican College, Levi Strauss & Co., Mt. Zion Hospital, and the Jewish Home for the Aged. Friedman was considered a mentor to architect Ray Kappe, with whom he became close friends. Kappe, also a former Emerson Junior High School student, had graduated from Berkeley in 1951 and returned to Southern California.

During Swatt's first summer break while still at Berkeley, he returned home and contacted several architecture firms seeking summer employment. Dan Dworsky and Kappe were two of the architects he contacted. Swatt took a job with Dworsky but maintained contact with Kappe, showing him his student projects whenever the opportunity presented itself.

Kappe, who started the Southern California Institute of Architecture (SCI-ARC) in 1972, remained a major influence on Swatt. Kappe's work and attitudes towards the profession, his superb sense of space, his use of exposed materials, and his ability to express structure in the simplest terms have shaped Swatt's work throughout his career (Fig. 3).

Fig 3 Kappe House

After graduating in 1970, Swatt designed his first house with Friedman for the Goldman family at Lake Tahoe. This early house explores the ideas of exposed structure and natural materials. The house hovers above the ground supported by exposed framing and steel girders that span between five cast-in-place concrete towers. In 1990 he was commissioned to design a guesthouse addition (Fig. 4).

Returning to Southern California in 1972, Swatt set up residence in Beverly Glen Canyon, across the street from architect Gordon Drake's own house. Swatt was familiar with the work of Drake through Friedman who considered Drake a hero. Drake's small post-war post-and-beam house won the Progressive Architecture Award in

1947. A well-known Julius Shulman photograph shows oversized French doors opening to an exterior living area, dissolving the boundary between indoor and outdoor space (Fig. 5). Swatt came into possession of a portfolio of original Shulman photographs that had been used in the book *The California Houses of Gordon Drake* by Douglas Baylis and Joan Perry. It is clear that the transparency and simple organization of Drake's work indirectly influenced Swatt. A wall of five bi-folding doors under a low soffit at Swatt's own house in Lafayette recalls Drake's connection to the

Fig 4 Goldman Vacation House

Fig 5 Drake House

outdoors, an unmistakable nod to one of the great post-war modernist architects.

At the beginning of what was to be his two years in Los Angeles, Swatt interviewed with Craig Ellwood and with Cesar Pelli at Gruen Associates. Swatt had heard Pelli lecture at Berkeley and was impressed by his eloquence on the subject of beauty. Swatt realized then that it was acceptable to be concerned with and to speak about the artistic aspects of architecture. Swatt became part of Gruen's design team, where he gained experience working on large, complex projects and learned about reflective materials, glass and metal, and the power of expressing clear plan organization. The Gruen's office at the time was a hothouse of design, with young talent from throughout the USA and abroad. The projects ranged from the United States Embassy in Tokyo, to the Pacific Design Center, the Los

Angeles Merchandise Mart, the San Bernardino City Hall, the Oakland City Center, and the Commons/Courthouse Center in Columbus, Indiana.

After two years working with Pelli, Swatt returned to Berkeley since work was slowing down at Gruen and Friedman had asked him to come back. From 1975 to 1977 Swatt taught studio classes at the university and opened his own office in Berkeley, starting with a speculative house, the Amito I House. His first effort was a 1500-square-foot house built for $30.00 per square foot. The tight stucco skin was an abstraction of the California adobe; it displayed the Southern California influence of Irving Gill's simplified facades. The house won for Swatt the AIA-Sunset Magazine design award (Fig. 6). The award helped establish Swatt's office and provided the credibility he needed to convince an investor to join him in a second speculative house, the Amito II House, also in Berkeley.

Amito II was a 1600-square-foot house built with an economical plywood skin. Perched on a hillside lot, the Amito II House won the national Plywood Design Award (Fig. 7). Both Amito I and Amito II burned to the ground in the Oakland-Berkeley fire of 1991. The local and international publicity generated by the awards for both houses enabled Swatt to attract his first client.

With the commission for the Paganelli House, Swatt took on architect Bernard Stein as a partner. Stein was also teaching at the university, and Swatt felt that a partnership might help jump-start the young firm. Together they produced a series of successful residential and commercial projects in Northern California.

The unbuilt Foster/Feldman House, an asymmetrical composition of solids and voids, shows the influence of Schindler's recently demolished 1929 Wolfe House on Catalina Island (Figs. 8, 9). Four levels are terraced into a steep hillside, much as the three levels of the Wolfe House cascade down the slope. Generous horizontal decks break up the strong vertical mass of the structure in both projects.

Fig 6 Amito I

The project gave Swatt an opportunity to work with a diverse material palette. Several different woods are used throughout the house. The richness of the exposed Douglas fir ceiling and the custom-built mahogany doors and windows warm the spaces, which are otherwise finished with predominately white walls and terrazzo floors.

The house expresses Swatt's keen interest in many of the same ideals as the early California modernists. Boundaries of indoor and outdoor space dissolve with floor-to-ceiling glass; corner windows with horizontal mullions and cantilevered decks break up the verticality of the structure. Built-in furniture becomes an integral part of the structure reducing the distraction that loose objects may impose on the

Fig 12 Carico House

environment. The living room couch in the Swatt House was made from glue-laminated beams set horizontally, inspired by the temporary bridges erected during construction.

The success of Swatt's own house has transformed his office, attracting a new type of client seeking livable modern architecture with a clear logic and strong organization. Swatt has returned to residential architecture with a renewed interest and passion. This has been a major shift in the focus of the Swatt office from a moderately large firm to a more hands-on 10-person firm headed up by Swatt, his long-time partner, Steven Stept, and two associates.

Swatt prefers to begin his residential projects by exploring solutions in three dimensions. Most projects begin with simple sketches of how the building program is distributed on the site. The building forms are not pre-determined, but instead evolve through three-dimensional studies that investigate the relation of the general parti to the site. In the most recent projects the first sketches are merely schematic suggestions of the organization of building elements. Form evolves through models and building elevations are only drawn after the design has fully evolved in model form.

Clients are brought into the process at every stage, from the earliest schematic to the final design. They sometimes even share the experience of 'remodeling' their model, as the design is refined.

Today Swatt Architects is a prolific practice with major commissions throughout California. The office is filled with study models of projects ranging from a single room modern tea house to residences as large as 14,000 square feet and a five-building residential loft project.

This new work builds on the belief that formal ideals need not be compromised to achieve architecture that works for people. Swatt Architects continues this commitment to balancing the social and the artistic aspects of architecture, the rational and the intuitive, the functional and the poetic, resulting in architecture that is both beautiful to look at and beautiful to live in.

Fig 13 Swatt House

Selected Projects

Swatt House
Lafayette, California
Design/Completion 1995/1997

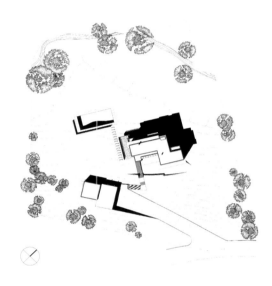

The Swatt House is the architect's own home. The 3800-square-foot residence is situated on a one-and-a-half-acre north-facing site, overlooking a creek, mature oak trees, and the hills of a regional park beyond. The project goals include a light and open interior suited to informal family life and entertaining, as well as a strong connection between the interior spaces and the natural environment.

The downward-sloping site, with access at the top and flat land at the bottom, suggested that the site be broken into three functional areas: carport/studio, main house, and pool. By detaching the house from the carport and locating it roughly halfway down the slope, the lower level gains direct access to the pool while the upper levels enjoy full exposure to views and daylight from all sides.

The interior of the home is organized around a glazed south-facing two-story spine, which defines circulation, admits maximum daylight, and provides access to the entry courtyard. Spaces at the main 'public' level are differentiated not through the use of walls and doors, but by materials, level changes, and built-in casework. To extend this openness to the exterior, five bi-folding glass doors open the spine and living areas to the entry courtyard, virtually eliminating the separation between indoor and outdoor spaces.

Opposite: West elevation **Above:** Site plan

17

Opposite: North elevation **Top right:** Entrance bridges **Bottom right:** Entrance detail

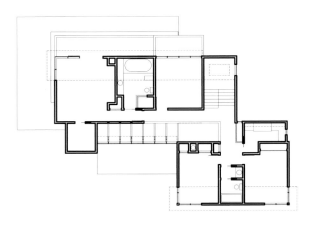

20

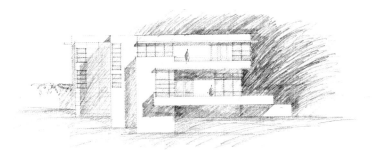

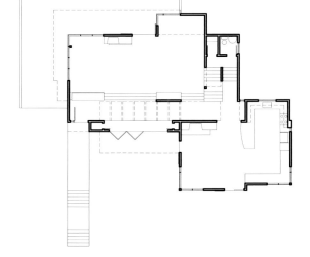

Top left: Model **Top right:** Upper level plan **Bottom left:** Early sketch of north elevation **Bottom right:** Main level plan **Opposite:** View from living room terrace

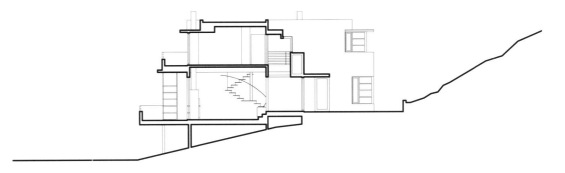

Opposite: View of living room from terrace **Top:** Living/dining room **Bottom:** Section

Opposite: Entry spine with skylight above **Left:** Living room detail
Right: Living room

Top: Kitchen and breakfast area **Bottom:** View from dining area
Opposite: View from living/dining room

Top: View from carport **Opposite:** Night view from pool terrace

Kohavi House

Portola Valley, California
Design/Completion 1997/2000

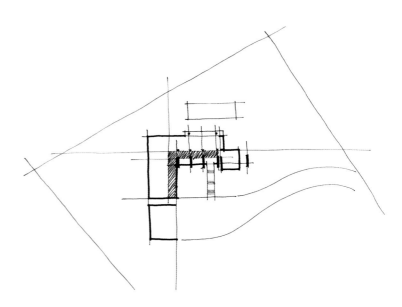

Set in the hills overlooking Palo Alto and San Francisco Bay, the design for the Kohavi House emphasizes the flow of space from indoors to outdoors, structural expression and connection to the land. The house is designed with an L-shaped plan which organizes the site, a one-and-a-half-acre east-facing knoll, into three distinct outdoor rooms: an entry court with low wood bridges on the western side, a children's play area on the northern side, and a future pool and terrace on the eastern side.

The plan is organized around a two-story circulation spine, articulated by four cast-in-place vertical concrete frames. Doors at either end of the spine provide access to the exterior and emphasize the connection of interior and exterior spaces. Adjacent to the circulation spine, the living-dining space is designed as a glass pavilion with a soaring, chevron-shaped, cantilevered roof that opens to panoramic views and visually extends interior space to the outdoors.

Above: Plan sketch **Opposite:** Entrance elevation **Following pages:** Overall view from south

34

Top: Southeast elevation **Bottom left:** Entrance court **Bottom right:** Exterior sketch
Opposite: Living/dining pavilion at night

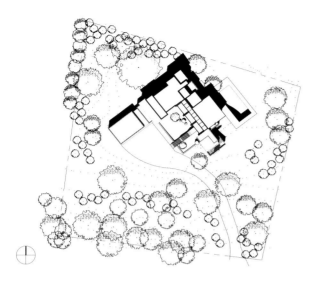

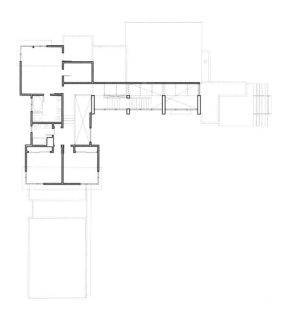

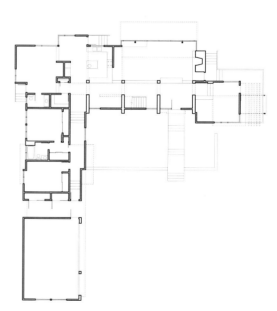

Top left: Site plan **Top right:** Upper level plan **Middle left:** Model
Bottom left: Model **Bottom right:** Lower level plan **Opposite:** Living room
from stair landing

Opposite: Living room **Top:** View
of stair from living room
Bottom: Living/dining room

Left: Kitchen **Middle:** Circulation spine looking
northwest **Right:** Stair detail **Opposite:** View from
living/dining pavilion

Palo Alto House

Palo Alto, California
Design/Completion 1998/2002

The owners, a young couple from Israel with four children, brought to this project a passion for architecture, a wealth of ideas collected over many years of contemplating their dream house, and a desire to create an artistic family home with unique materials and details. The result, a true collaboration between client and architect, is a lively composition of dynamic spaces, rich materials and intricate detailing.

The site is a typical suburban corner lot, selected more for its proximity to outstanding schools than for its unique physical features. One of the challenges of this site involved the creation of private outdoor areas, with strong visual and functional connections to the interior, while maintaining privacy from the street.

The planning for this 6000-square-foot house started with the concept of dividing the building program into two major wings: a 'public' and adult wing, and a 'private' guest and children's wing. A dramatic double-height gallery links the two wings and contains the principal horizontal and vertical circulation for the house. To provide privacy, the gallery space is opaque on the street side. On the garden side, a two-story glass curtain wall contrasts with the cast-in-place concrete street-side wall, dramatically extending interior space to the exterior and providing visual links between the wings of the house.

The interior features contrasting materials and surprising details. A glass floor bridge provides access to a library overlooking the living room, with the transparent floor allowing light from a linear skylight to illuminate the room below. Within the central gallery a maple clad stair, with a thin internal steel frame, floats between the walls of the gallery and pirouettes around a frameless glass wall suspended from stainless steel rods.

Left: View from kitchen **Oppposite:** Front entry courtyard at night

Opposite: Entrance **Top:** View from kitchen terrace
Bottom: Gallery from rear garden

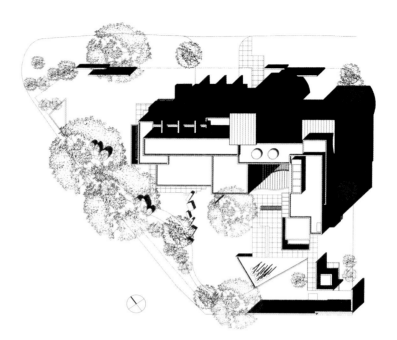

Opposite left: Rear garden **Opposite right:** Site plan **Left:** Upper level plan
Right: Lower level plan

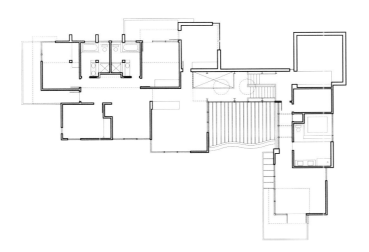

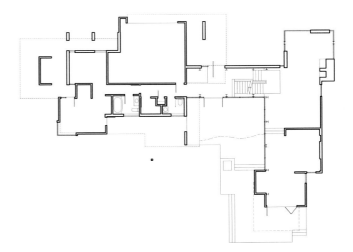

Top: Kitchen **Bottom:** Kitchen **Opposite:** Dining room with library and glass bridge above

Top: View of rear garden and gallery stair **Opposite:** Master bedroom

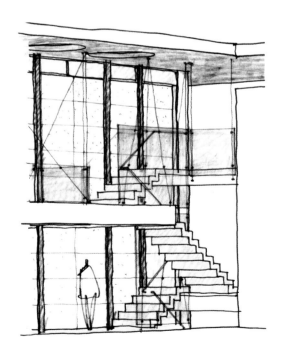

Opposite: Gallery Top left: Stair detail
Top right: Stair detail Bottom right: Stair sketch

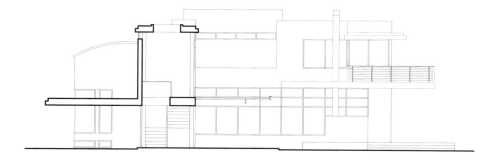

Top: View of kitchen/dining area at night
Bottom: Section **Opposite:** Gallery at night

Greason House

Lafayette, California
Design/Completion 1999/2002

The Greason House is a small project, adding 1350 square feet to a 3300-square-foot 1970s boxy suburban home. Functionally, the project includes a new upper level guest/study wing over a new garage, tied to the main house by a new skylit passageway.

As the project unfolded, it became clear to the architect and owner that the project's location, adjacent to the entrance and immediately visible from the approaching private drive, created an opportunity to transform the entire look and feel of the house. The design is an exercise in achieving maximum impact from a few well-considered modifications.

Design cues were taken from the existing architecture, with existing vertical slot windows in the living room reappearing as new windows in the addition and as voids between three new garden walls. The new upstairs guestroom opens to a balcony which overlooks the private pool area, while the study overlooks a new Zen-like entrance with a fountain, bamboo, river rocks and low retaining walls which highlight an existing large maple tree. At the ground level, a new cantilevered roof overhang has been added to define the entrance. Removal of existing warped wood roof fascia boards and re-sheathing of the entire building in white sand finished stucco unifies the building forms and completes the aesthetic transformation.

Opposite: Entrance roof overhang detail
Right: South view of entrance

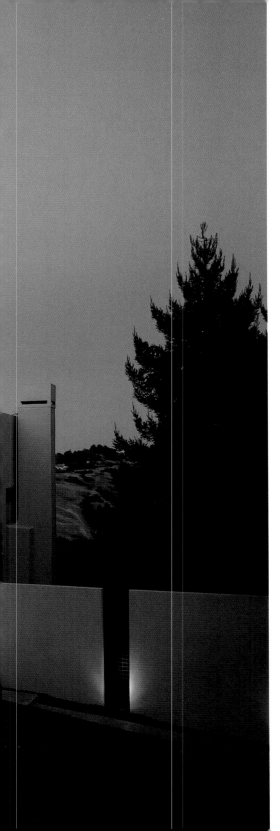

Opposite: Overall view from southwest
Top: Entrance from northwest
Bottom: Exterior detail

Woodland House

Kentfield, California
Design/Completion 1998/2001

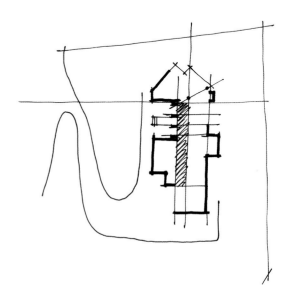

The Woodland House, located on a steep and heavily wooded site, is designed to maximize views and access to the surrounding natural landscape of magnificent forested hills.

The design of this 5000-square-foot house relies on a long U-shaped plan, with the entrance in a private courtyard at the center. Internally, the house is organized along a dramatic two-story circulation spine that connects all major spaces. The spine is designed with a linear skylight above the two-story portion and a continuous clerestory above the one-story entrance to flood the interior with natural light.

The living and dining area, located opposite the entrance courtyard, has been sculpted with a gentle up-sloping ceiling that dramatically cantilevers to the exterior, opening up views to the trees and connecting the house with the outdoors.

Above: Plan sketch **Opposite:** Entrance courtyard looking south

Opposite: View of breakfast area and living room from rear yard **Left:** Entrance courtyard **Above:** Overall view from southeast

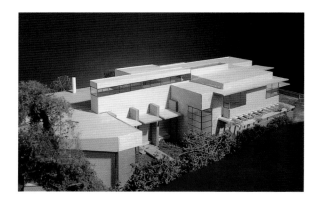

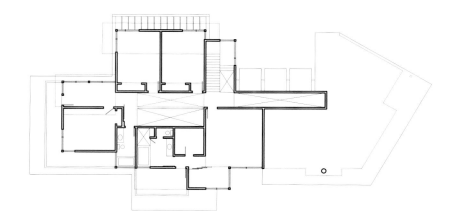

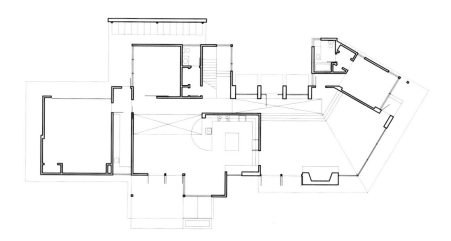

Top left: Model **Top right:** Upper level plan
Bottom left: Model **Bottom right:** Lower level
plan **Opposite:** Entry

Opposite: Living/dining room **Top left:** Circulation spine with skylight above **Top right:** Living/dining room **Bottom left:** Stair

Opposite: Dining room **Top left:** View from driveway **Right:** Living room at night **Bottom left:** View of breakfast area with master bedroom above

Conrad House
Sausalito, California
Design/Completion 1999/2002

The Conrad House is built over the footprint of a 1950s residence by noted Bay Area modernist Roger Lee that over the years had suffered irreparable structural damage. The new design doubles the area of the house to 2700 square feet while maintaining the original emphasis on the expressive use of wood and the distribution of public and private spaces.

This new residence for a young couple works with its hillside site by providing direct access to outdoor areas and taking advantage of views of San Francisco Bay and Mt. Tamalpais. The owners expressed a strong desire that wherever possible the design utilized natural materials left in their original state.

The new design retains the spirit of the original exterior and interior through its expressive use of wood structure and finishes. Strip windows and cedar siding emphasize the horizontality of the design, extending the lines of the house into the site, and helping nestle the house into the hillside. Post-and-beam construction reveals the structure of the

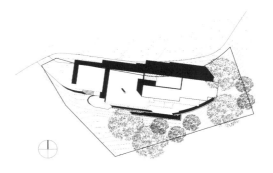

house and articulates the grid upon which it is based. Tongue and groove cedar soffits visually connect interior spaces to decks and terraces beyond.

All major rooms are situated on the northern side of the house to take advantage of panoramic views of San Francisco Bay and Mt. Tamalpais. An expansive double-height stair hall on the southern side of the house connects all major rooms and acts as a counterpoint to the horizontality of the rest of the design. This hall has a floor-to-ceiling window facing the hillside beyond that allows sunlight, filtered through a canopy of mature live oaks, to penetrate deep into the house.

Opposite: North elevation at night **Above:** Site plan

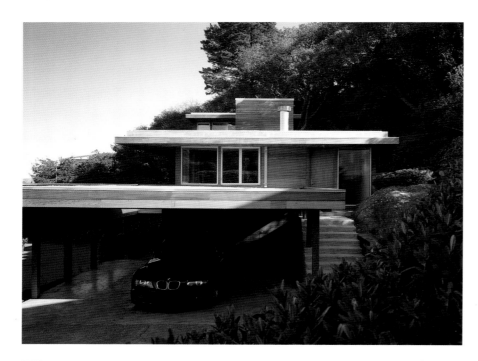

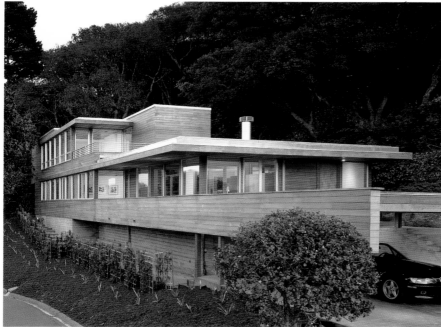

Top: West elevation **Bottom:** Overall view from northwest
Opposite: Entry at night

74

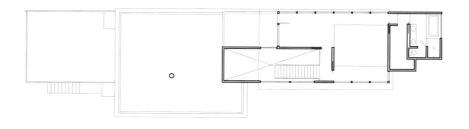

Top left: Exterior detail **Top right:** Upper level plan
Bottom right: Lower level plan **Opposite:** Living room

Opposite: Kitchen **Left:** Dining area and stair **Right:** Stair and rear garden

Above: View from master bedroom **Left:** Stair from rear garden **Opposite:** Master bedroom and sitting area

The Icehouse

Headquarters of Levi Strauss & Co.
San Francisco, California
Design/Completion 1990/1993

The Icehouse is San Francisco's largest masonry complex, built in 1914 to manufacture ice for the city's fishing industry. In 1990 Levi Strauss & Co. purchased The Icehouse, and Swatt Architects was charged with turning the 200,000-square-foot complex into part of their corporate headquarters. The design was to reflect the company's culture and the style of its products—practical, flexible, understated and comfortable with a sense of uniqueness and quality.

The complex consists of two brick-clad and timber-framed buildings, five and seven stories high, connected by a five-level steel and glass bridge. In order to make the three building elements function efficiently for a single tenant, each of the three building elements has been reconfigured on the interior with connecting loop circulation systems that weave

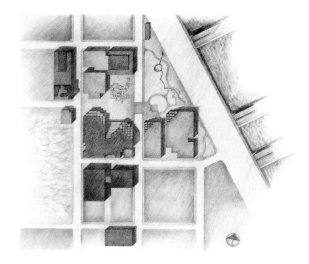

through a forest of timber columns. Central services are located inside the circulation loops, and workspaces are located on the perimeter. The plan organization is simple, understandable, flexible, and reserves maximum natural light and views for employee workspaces.

The design celebrates what is old, unusual and historic about The Icehouse. Brick walls, timber columns and beams, and steel seismic bracing have been uncovered and left exposed. New light furnishings and finishes with sophisticated and minimal detailing contrast with the heavy historical elements. The Icehouse now speaks of two ages: the period of San Francisco's bustling northern waterfront fishing industry, and today's modern Bay Area corporate environment.

Opposite left: Icehouse II from northeast Opposite right: Site plan Right: Bridge between Icehouse buildings

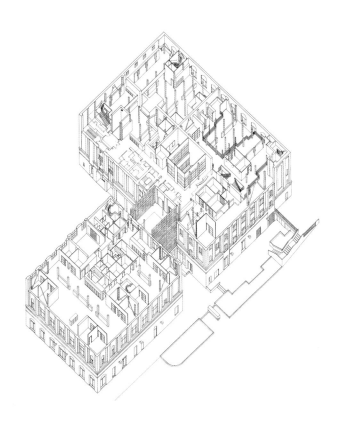

Left: Bridge **Right**: Axonometric **Opposite**: Bridge lounge

84

Left: Lightwell in Icehouse I **Right:** Conference room with lightwell above **Opposite top:** Bridge section **Opposite bottom:** Icehouse I section

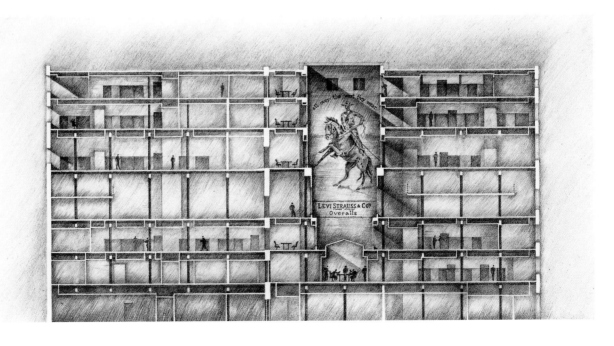

Opposite: Bridge lunch room **Left:** Lunch room detail
Above: Lunch room detail

Background: 4th floor mezzanine of Icehouse I
Opposite: Mezzanine detail **Left:** 4th floor of Icehouse I
Right: Bridge stair detail

Above: Typical circulation loop **Opposite:** Credit Union

Free Speech Movement Café

University of California, Berkeley
Design/Completion 1998/2000

The Free Speech Movement Café at the University of California, Berkeley, campus has been designed to pay tribute to what Chancellor Robert M. Berdahl has called 'the firestorm that the FSM created across the nation'. The café exhibits articles, quotations, literature, photos, and a giant mural of the events that set off the Free Speech Movement in Berkeley in 1964, and also celebrates current social activism with news, monitors, computer access to the FSM and other websites, and an LED display designed to announce current events from a news wire service.

The café, with indoor and outdoor seating for 250, was voted the most popular gathering place on the UC Berkeley campus. The design uses warm and natural materials, including floating wood ceiling planes and a custom wood storefront system, contrasted against the cool concrete finishes of the building shell, to create spaces which are as comfortable and inviting as a 1960s Berkeley coffeehouse.

Right: Sign leading to café entrance **Opposite:** Café entrance

Opposite: Overall interior view **Top:** Entrance sketch **Left:** Overall interior view **Above:** Interior sketch

Background: Café seating in front of mural Opposite: Interior view looking west
Below: Students at entrance courtyard

Mayol House

Escalon, California
Design/Completion 1999/2004

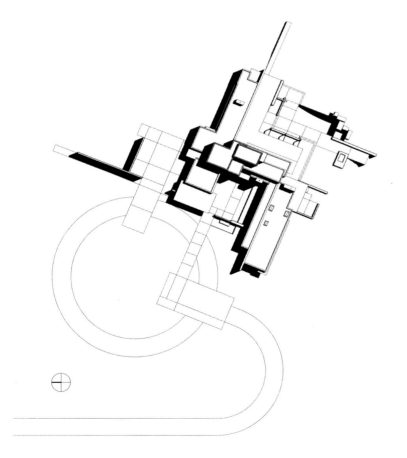

This house has been designed to take full advantage of its magnificent site in California's Central Valley. Perched on the edge of a cliff, the 7400-square-foot home is accessed by a long entry drive through a 25-acre walnut orchard. The design affords uninterrupted views of the Stanislaus River and wetlands below as well as direct access to outdoor living spaces such as courtyards, a pool, spa and a new three-acre fishing pond.

The predominately one-story design is organized around a Z-shaped circulation spine that creates two distinct courtyards, one a formal entry court, the other a series of informal terraces for relaxation and entertainment. The spine links the bedroom and informal family living wings to a more formal, central living/dining pavilion. Strong connections to the exterior are created through the use of ample glazing as well as doors that give direct access to terraces from all major spaces. Expansive areas of glass provide for maximum daylighting, while the use of deep overhangs protects the interior from the intense heat of the Central Valley summer.

Left: Site plan **Opposite:** Model

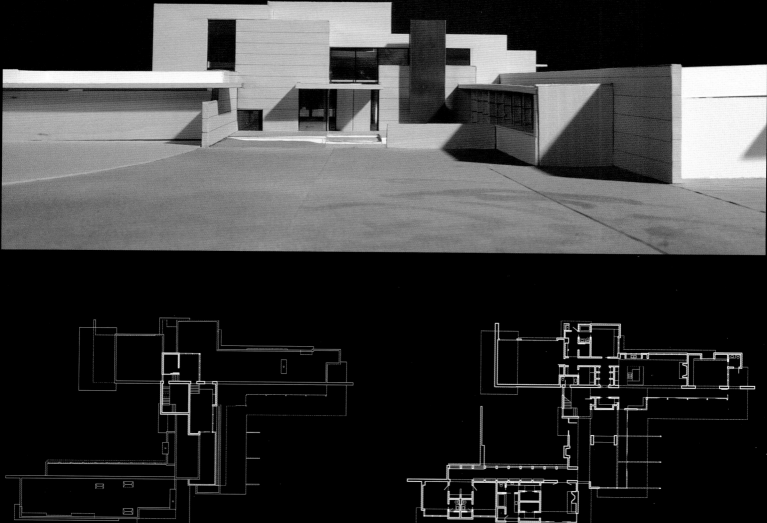

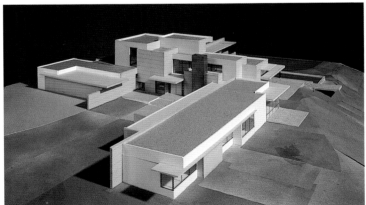

Opposite top: Model view of entrance courtyard **Opposite bottom
left:** Upper level plan **Opposite bottom right:** Lower level plan
Above: Interior sketch **Right:** Model

Shimmon House I
Los Altos Hills, California
Design 2000-2001

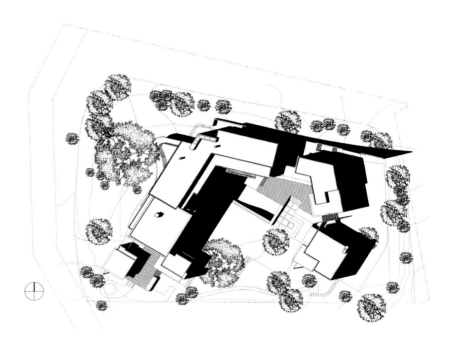

The Shimmon House I is located on a gently sloping one-and-a-half-acre knoll, bordered on three sides by a narrow access road which serves a small neighborhood of surrounding houses. A major goal of the project has been to create, using the building forms, private and protected exterior spaces for enjoyment of the outdoors.

The building program for this 14,300-square-foot house has been configured into three connected wings: a 'public' great room, kitchen and dining wing; a library and guestroom wing; and a gymnasium wing. Anchoring the ends of the U-shaped plan are a home office and a two-story guesthouse. Circulation occurs on the courtyard side of all major spaces, and is articulated with linear wood soffits which extend from interior corridors through mahogany-framed glass curtain walls to the exterior. All major ground floor spaces have large sliding glass panels which blur the distinction between indoor and outdoor space. The private courtyard is defined by the building form, and is designed for maximum family use with outdoor cooking and dining areas, spa, flower garden, fire pit, raised wood viewing decks, lawn volleyball court, and infinity edge swimming pool.

Opposite: Site plan **Top left:** Model view of
courtyard **Top right:** Model view of courtyard
Bottom: Exterior sketch

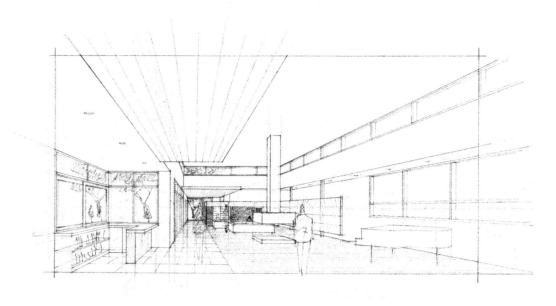

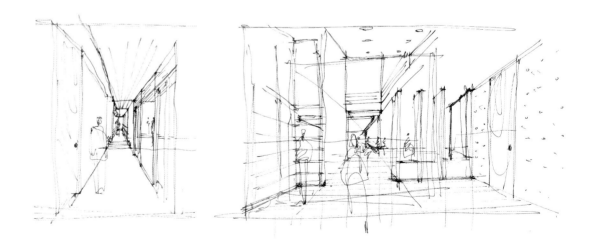

Top left: Model view of initial design scheme
Top right: Interior sketch **Middle left:** Model view
of initial design scheme **Bottom middle & bottom
right:** Sketches **Opposite top left:** Upper level plan
Opposite right: Model view of initial design
scheme **Opposite bottom left:** Lower level plan

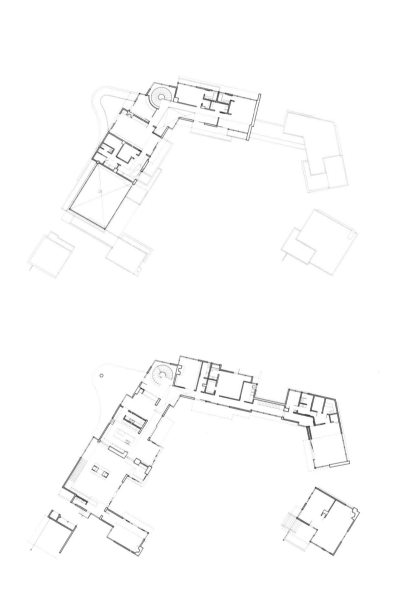

GreenCity Lofts
Oakland/Emeryville, California
Design/Completion 1999/2004

GreenCity Lofts is located on the Oakland/Emeryville, California, border and is comprised of 62 loft condominiums in five buildings ranging from three to five stories in height over structured parking.

Many elements of the design, such as high ceilings and large expanses of glass, reflect the live/work loft building type while at the same time blending with a diverse neighborhood that contains residential, commercial and light industrial uses.

GreenCity Lofts is one of the first multi-family projects in the nation designed according to 'green' principles. This transit oriented, urban infill project focuses on the economical use of recycled and sustainably harvested materials, energy efficiency, healthy interior environments, and native landscaping.

Above: Model **Opposite top:** Overall view from northwest
Opposite bottom: Sketch

Opposite: Plan Right: West elevation Below: North elevation

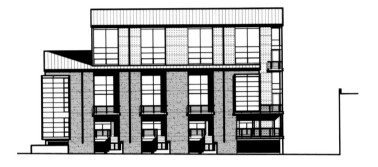

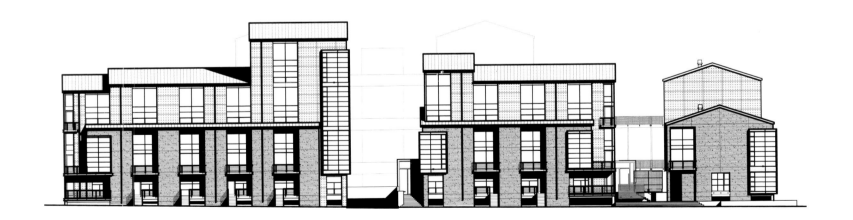

Morley House

Lafayette, California
Design/Completion 2003/2005

The Morley House is a new 5465-square-foot residence located on a one-and-a-half-acre wooded site with a gentle cross slope that leads to a stream at the southern edge of the property.

The design is an L-shaped plan with three grade levels that step with the contours of the land. The plan creates an entrance and motor court on the northern side of the house, articulated by a series of stepped, opaque planes that provide privacy from the street. The southern side, by contrast, is almost entirely glazed to provide access and views to a private terrace, swimming pool, and the creek beyond.

The form of the house consists of folded planes, sheathed in redwood, interlocking with a series of stucco masses that step with the land. The redwood planes, where they fold through or around the stucco masses, create glazed voids that are protected by broad overhangs.

Right: Plan sketch **Opposite top:** Model **Opposite bottom left:** Upper level plan **Opposite bottom right:** Lower level plan

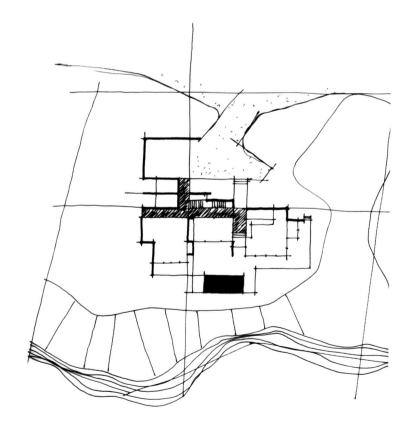

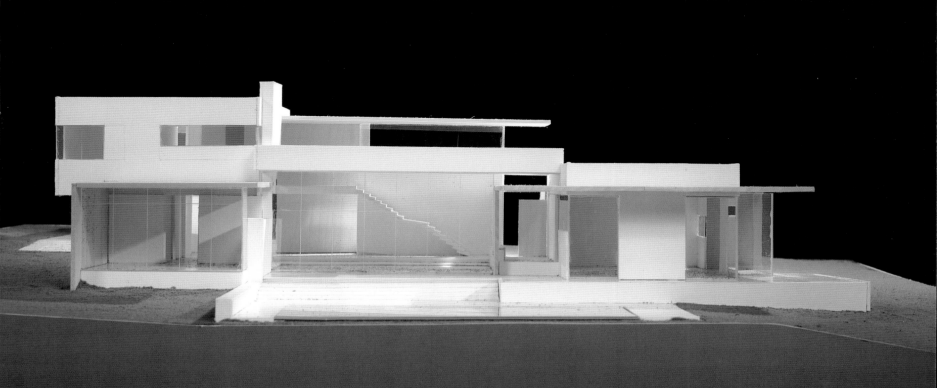

Opposite top: East elevation Opposite bottom: Model view of south
elevation Below: Section Bottom: Entrance and living room sketches

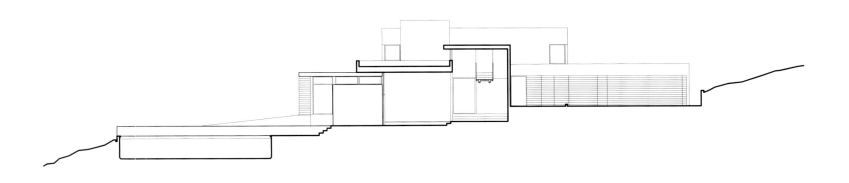

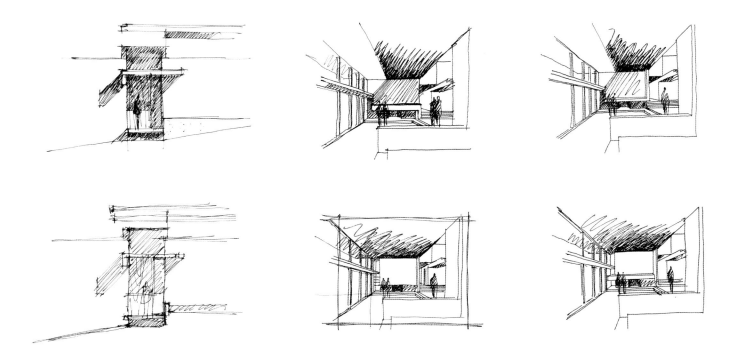

Tea Houses
Silicon Valley, California
Design/Completion 2002/2004

Perched on the edge of a three-acre canyon site within groves of redwood and maple trees, these three tea house pavilions have been designed to compliment a 6000 square foot main house which has been extensively remodeled by Swatt Architects.

The structures are steel and glass 'lanterns' suspended above the hillside between cast-in-place concrete towers. The larger of the two structures, consisting of two pavilions linked by a skylit concrete service space, provides spaces for work and sleep remote from the house. The smaller pavilion, for meditation, is located on a lower earth bench about 35 feet from its larger sibling.

The frameless glazing of the pavilions allows uninterrupted views of the canyon and city below by day and will illuminate the structures as glowing light boxes in the garden at night.

Right: Plan/section sketch **Opposite top left & right:** Model
Opposite bottom: Site plan

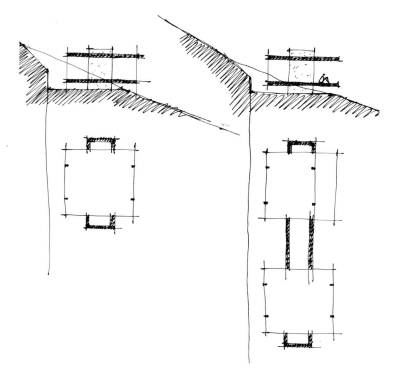

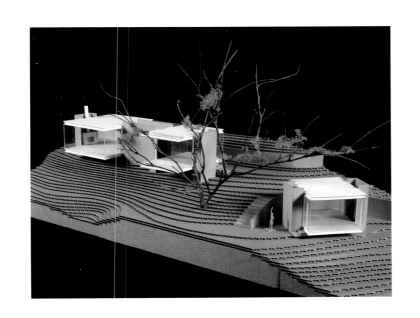

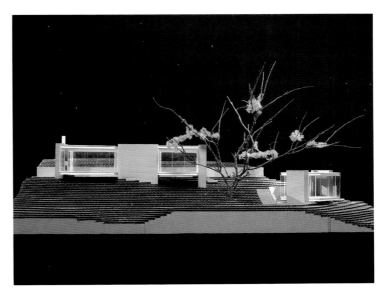

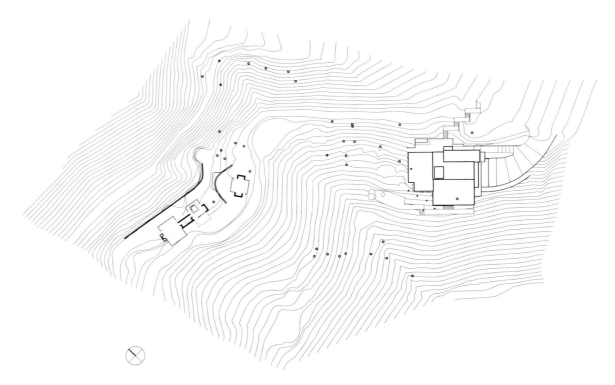

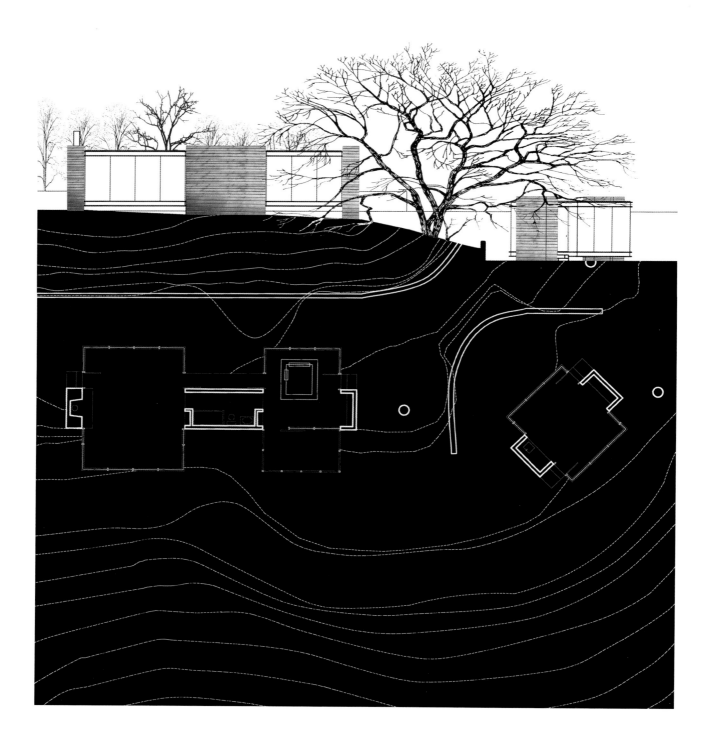

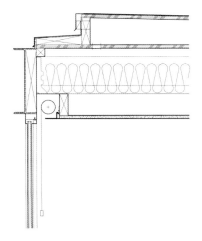

Opposite: Plan/elevation **Top left:** Detail **Top right:** Model
Left: Model/montage detail

Project Credits

Swatt House
Project team: Robert Swatt, Cristina Poblete, and Tom Hunter
Consultants: Ingraham-DeJesse Associates, structural;
Architectural Lighting Design, lighting

Kohavi House
Project team: Robert Swatt, David Burton, and Steven Stept
Consultants: Tek Pe Engineers, structural; Ron Herman, landscape
Contractor: Cowan & Gentry Construction

Palo Alto House
Project team: Robert Swatt, Steven Stept, David Burton,
Cristina Poblete, Ken Chan, Sarina Bowen, and Paul Martinez
Consultants: Tek Pe Engineers, structural; Tipping Mar
& Associates, structural; MPA Design, landscape
Contractor: Van Catlin Construction

Greason House
Project team: Robert Swatt, Steven Stept, and Kee-Ree Roh
Consultants: Applied Structural Associates, structural;
Ron Herman, landscape
Contractor: Van Catlin Construction

Woodland House
Project team: Robert Swatt, David Burton, Steven Stept,
Ken Chan, and Gregory Holah
Consultant: Barry H. Welliver Engineering, structural;
Antonia Bava, landscape
Contractor: Juan Calmell

Conrad House
Project team: Robert Swatt, David Burton, Alden Marsh,
and Christopher Korbuly
Consultant: Tek Pe Engineers, structural
Contractor: Creative Energy Corporation

The Icehouse
Project team: Robert Swatt, Steven Stept, Eric Kopelson,
Adrienne Kay, David Finn, Sun Lee-Hong, Fred Reiber,
Scott Colson, Roger Ricketts, Joanne Powell, I. Flynn Rosenthal,
Kasia Kowalska-Ekstrand, Stan Ogden, Michael Buncick,
David Christopher Loye, Tom Hunter, Susan Aitken,
Duncan Griffin, Tim Firman, Elizabeth Peck Repass,
Jeffrey Acuff, William Curtis, Karyn Gabriel, Janet Robb,
and Thomas Worden

Consultants: Forell/Elsesser Engineers, structural;
Glumac International, mechanical; The Engineering Enterprise,
electrical; Architectural Lighting Design, lighting; Clara Igonda,
finishes
Contractor: R.N. Field Construction

Free Speech Movement Café
Project team: Robert Swatt, Steven Stept, Sun Lee-Hong,
Kee Ree-Roh, and Harry Matte (exhibits and graphics)
Consultants: Ingraham-DeJesse Associates, structural; MHC
Engineers, mechanical; The Engineering Enterprise, electrical;
Architectural Lighting Design, lighting
Contractor: J.R. Griffin Construction

Mayol House
Project team: Robert Swatt, Matthew Mosey,
and Christopher Korbuly
Consultants: CB Engineering, structural; Westfall Design Studio,
landscape; Chris Reed Design, interiors

Shimmon House I
Project team: Robert Swatt, Matthew Mosey, Eunice Lin,
Wanda Lieberman, Ken Chan, and Ken Powelson
Consultants: Yu Engineering, structural; Blasen Landscape
Architecture, landscape; Architectural Lighting Design, lighting

GreenCity Lofts
Project team: Robert Swatt, David Burton, Greg Holah,
Kasia Kowalska-Ekstrand, Eunice Lin, Paul Martinez,
Hiromi Ogawa, Ken Powelson, Jeanie Fan, and Kristin Personett
Consultants: KPFF, structural; MPA Design, landscape

Morley House
Project team: Robert Swatt, David Burton, Eser Turan,
and Kristin Personett
Consultants: Yu Engineering, structural; Patricia O'Brien,
landscape

Tea Houses
Project team: Robert Swatt, Steven Stept, Hiromi Ogawa,
and Jeanie Fan
Consultants: Yu Engineering, structural; Connie Wong, interiors

Biographies

Robert Swatt

Born in 1947, Robert Swatt grew up in Los Angeles where he was exposed to the works of California's early modern masters and gained an appreciation of architecture at an early age. He received his education at the University of California, Berkeley, graduating with honors in 1970.

Robert Swatt opened his own firm in 1975. From 1977 to 1984 he was a principal of Swatt & Stein Architects, and in 1984 founded Swatt Architects in San Francisco. Prior to starting his own firm, he worked with Howard A. Friedman in San Francisco and Cesar Pelli in Los Angeles. From 1975 to 1977 he taught architectural design at the University of California, Berkeley, where he has also served as a Director of the College of Environmental Design Alumni Association and was a founding member of the Distinguished Alumni Awards committee. He has lectured at the San Francisco Museum of Modern Art and the Monterey Design Conference, and exhibited work at the Monterey Design Conference, Modernbook/Gallery 494, LIMN, the San Francisco AIA, the University of California, Berkeley, and the Cooper-Hewitt Museum in New York. In 1992 Robert Swatt was elected to the College of Fellows of the American Institute of Architects.

The firm of Swatt Architects, based in Emeryville, California, has built a reputation for design excellence covering an extraordinary variety of project types. Recent projects include highly acclaimed residences throughout the Bay Area; a sustainable loft housing project in Emeryville; a new campus for the Reutlinger Center for Jewish Living; hospitality centers and exhibits for Beaulieu Vineyards, Glen Ellen Winery, Codorniu Napa, Wellington Vineyards and Wildhorse Winery; and the Free Speech Movement Café at the University of California, Berkeley. The firm has been recognized with over 35 design awards, including nine awards from the American Institute of Architects and a National Honor Award for The Icehouse, Headquarters of Levi Strauss & Co..

Articles on Robert Swatt's work have been published in Architecture, Architectural Record, Domus, GA Houses, Hinge, Interior Design, the New York Times, Process Architecture, Progressive Architecture, Wallpaper, and other journals and magazines in the USA and abroad.

Steven Stept

A Pennsylvania native, born in 1961, Steven Stept attended The Pennsylvania State University where he received a Bachelor of Architecture degree in 1986. Following his passion for modern design, he joined the firm of Swatt Architects in 1987, became an associate in 1988, and was named a principal in 1995. Prior to joining Swatt Architects, he worked with Hellmuth, Obata & Kassabaum (HOK) in Washington, DC, and several small design firms in San Francisco and Pennsylvania.

Steven Stept has managed numerous award-winning projects for corporate, institutional, and private clients. His projects have been published in Designer's West, Contract Design, Western Interiors and Design, Sunset Magazine, Architectural Record, and other journals and magazines in the USA and abroad, and exhibited at Modernbook/Gallery 494 and the University of California, Berkeley.

Steven Stept is a member of the American Institute of Architects, and has served as a special events coordinator for the San Francisco Museum of Modern Art and as president of the San Francisco Bay Area Chapter of the Pennsylvania State Alumni Association.

Associates & Employees

Principals

Robert Swatt, FAIA

Steven Stept, AIA

Associates

David Burton, AIA

Matthew Mosey, AIA

Current and Former Staff

Jeffrey Acuff

Scott Adams

Susan Aitken

Carlos Alvarez

Sarina Bowen

Michael Buncick

Ken Chan

Alejandra Cisneros

Ann Rollins Clark

Scott Colson

William Curtis

Crellan Duffy

Michael Duran

Jeanie Fan

David Finn

Tim Firman

Karyn Gabriel

Thalia Georgopoulos

Judy Greif

Duncan Griffin

Alice Hall

Gregory Holah

Sun Lee-Hong

Beth Hopper

Tom Hunter

Marcelo Igonda

Geoffrey James

Adrienne Kay

Eric Kopelson

Christopher Korbuly

Kasia Kowalska-Ekstrand

Stacey Lee

Wendy Lewis

Wanda Lieberman

Eunice Lin

David Christopher Loye

Alden Marsh

Paul Martinez

Katie McCamant

John McCarthy

Constance McKnight

Scott Min

Wendy Narlock

Hiromi Ogawa

Stan Ogden

Julie Pereira

Mark Perry

Kristin Personett

Cristina Poblete

Jay Powell

Joanne Powell

Ken Powelson

Fred Reiber

Elizabeth Peck Repass

Roger Ricketts

Janet Robb

Kee-Ree Roh

I. Flynn Rosenthal

Ruth Siegel

Vicki Simon

Susan Snow

Guy Snyder

Eileen Sullivan

Stuart Thompson

Eser Turan

Vera Westergaard

Thomas Worden

Selected Chronology

Robert Swatt Architect

1975

Swatt/Luckham/Bennett (Amito I) House, Berkeley, California

1976

Swatt/Everts (Amito II) House, Berkeley, California

Swatt & Stein Architects

1976

Paganelli House, Oakland, California

1977

Overlook Houses, Walnut Creek, California

Swahlen House Addition, San Rafael, California

Competition for an Energy Efficient Office Building, Sacramento, California

Brodsky House, Scotts Valley, California

Foster/Feldman House, Berkeley, California

1978

Conroy House Terraces, Berkeley, California

Crocker Bank Retail Banking Headquarters, San Francisco, California

Sommers House, Sausalito, California

Weissberg House, Oakland, California

1979

Wrubel House Addition, Berkeley, California

Riback/Steffen House, Oakland, California

Carico House, San Francisco, California

Taunton House, Lake Tahoe, California

Ionic Building, Oakland, California

Laio House, Berkeley, California

1980

New Entrance to the Japanese Tea Garden, Golden Gate Park, San Francisco, California

H.I.S. Building, Japantown, San Francisco, California

Miller House, Santa Cruz, California

Mirabeau Greenhouse Restaurant, Oakland, California

1981

Crocker Banks, Salinas and Sacramento, California

Prusinski House Addition, Orinda, California

Barratt Studio Solo, Sacramento, California

Okabe Sports, San Francisco, California

Iroha Restaurant, San Francisco, California

1982

Gerson Bakar Greenhouse, San Francisco, California

Barratt Infill Housing, Sacramento and Emeryville, California

Heilbron Square, Sacramento, California

Bank of America, San Francisco International Airport, San Francisco, California

1983

Bill Graham House Addition, Corte Madera, California

Swatt Architects

1984

Wilsey Conservatory, San Francisco, California

Koret Manufacturing Plant, Price, Utah

Treat Executive Center Interiors, Walnut Creek, California

Koshland House, Berkeley, California

1985

Herrick/Kunitz House, Berkeley, California

UC Berkeley Business School, Feasibility Study and Schematic Design, Berkeley, California

Bauch House, Belvedere, California

Osgood/Coppola House, San Francisco, California

Kingsley House Addition, San Francisco, California

1986

Thom House, Woodside, California

Strunsky House Remodel, San Francisco, California

Levi Strauss & Co. Finishing Center, San Francisco, California

1987

Treble House Addition, Palo Alto, California

Jewish Home for the Aged Boutique, San Francisco, California

Levi Strauss & Co. Regional Sales Offices, Atlanta, Georgia

Schrag/Marinoff Studio, Berkeley, California

Levi Strauss & Co. Finishing Center, San Antonio, Texas

1988

Friedman House Addition, San Francisco, California

Plaza Café Remodel, Carmel, California

American Tin Cannery Master Plan, Pacific Grove, California

Levi Strauss & Co. Distribution Shipping Area, Henderson, Nevada

Levi Strauss & Co. Conference Center, San Francisco, California

Abraham House, Orinda, California

Levi Strauss & Co. Master Plan, San Francisco, California

Bauch Beach House, Stinson Beach, California

1989

Goldman House Addition, San Francisco, California

Esther & Jacques Reutlinger Community for Jewish Living, Danville, California

Levi Strauss & Co. History Museum, San Francisco, California

1990

The Icehouse – Levi Strauss & Co. Headquarters, San Francisco, California

Haas Ranch House Remodel, Big Timber, Montana

Haas House Solarium, San Francisco, California

Goldman Vacation House, Lake Tahoe, California

Levi Strauss & Co. Showrooms and Regional Sales Offices, Los Angeles, California

1991

Levi Strauss & Co. Showrooms and Regional Sales Offices, San Francisco, California

Levi Strauss & Co. East Bay Offices, Walnut Creek, California

Blatteis House Addition, Oakland, California

Adcock House, Oakland, California

Barney House, Oakland, California

Levi Strauss & Co. Data Center, San Francisco, California

Swatt House Remodel, Oakland, California

1992

Richard & Rhoda Goldman Fund Offices, San Francisco, California

Peter & Mimi Haas Fund Offices, San Francisco, California

Evelyn & Walter Haas Jr. Fund Offices, San Francisco, California

Columbia Foundation Offices, San Francisco, California

Larsen/Wong House, Oakland, California

Icehouse Alley, San Francisco, California

1993

Wells Fargo Branch Bank, Fresno, California

544 2nd Street Building Alterations, San Francisco, California

Koshland House Addition, Lafayette, California

UC Berkeley Evans Hall Classrooms, Berkeley, California

1994

BR Cohn Winery Hospitality Center Study, Glen Ellen, California

Ocean View House, Oakland, California

Growers Square Renovations, Walnut Creek, California

Stanford University Dormitories, Stanford, California

Mikimoto Boutique, San Francisco, California

Abbey House Alterations, San Francisco, California

UC Berkeley Telecommunications Offices, Berkeley, California

Dominican College Classroom Standards, San Rafael, California

1995

Swatt House, Lafayette, California

Levi Strauss & Co. Saddleman Building Renovation, San Francisco, California

Glen Ellen Winery Tasting Room and History Center, Glen Ellen, California

Fritzi California Master Plan, San Francisco, California

Pitney Bowes Offices, San Francisco, California

Chetkowski House Addition, Piedmont, California

UC Berkeley Memorial Stadium Club Room, Berkeley, California

1996

Levi Strauss & Co. Showrooms and Regional Sales Offices, San Francisco, California

UC Davis Laboratory Alterations, Davis, California

1997

UC Davis Recreation Hall Upgrades, Davis, California

UC Davis Chancellor's Conference Room, Davis, California

Kohavi/Lace House, Portola Valley, California

Wellington Vineyards Tasting Room, Glen Ellen, California

Stark/Drayer House Addition, Oakland, California

1998

Meridian Winery Exhibit, Paso Robles, California

UC Berkeley Free Speech Movement Café, Berkeley, California

UC Berkeley Microcomputer Center, Berkeley, California

Palo Alto House, Palo Alto, California

Codorniu-Napa Carneros Museum, Napa, California

Wildhorse Winery Tasting Room and Hospitality Center Design, Templeton, California

Crossbrook Drive Homes, Moraga, California

Woodland House, Kentfield, California

1999

Mayol House, Escalon, California

UC Berkeley Media Resources Center, Berkeley, California

St. Mark's Episcopal Church Restoration, Berkeley, California

Rosen House Remodel, Lafayette, California

UC Davis Bainer Hall Laboratory Renovations, Davis, California

Kamat House Addition and Remodel, San Carlos, California

Greason House Addition, Lafayette, California

UC Davis Mrak Hall Administration Building Interiors, Davis, California

GreenCity Lofts, Oakland/Emeryville, California

Nelson Communications, Sacramento, California

Vignos House Addition, Orinda, California

Hoffman Houses, Lafayette, California

Conrad House, Sausalito, California

2000

Lea House Addition, Orinda, California

CBS Marketwatch.com, San Francisco, California

Shimmon House I, Los Altos Hills, California

Hoffman Secluded Place House, Lafayette, California

2001

Palo Alto Guest House, Palo Alto, California

Gradman House, Inverness, California

2002

Sackett/Mohsenin House, Ross, California

Shimmon House II, Los Altos Hills, California

St. John's Episcopal Church School, Ross, California

Orr House, Saratoga, California

Tea Houses, Silicon Valley, California

2003

Lukaszewicz/Moayeri House Addition, Hillsborough, California

Chang/Worzel House Remodel, San Francisco, California

Morley House, Lafayette, California

King House Addition and Pool House, Lafayette, California

Selected Publications

Books

1000 Architects, Images Publishing Group, Melbourne, Australia, 2004

Another 100 Of The World's Best Houses, Images Publishing Group, Melbourne, Australia, 2003

Cook, Jeffrey, *Award Winning Passive Solar House Designs*, Garden Way, 1984

Futagawa, Yukio, *GA Houses 64*, Tokyo, 2000

Health Spaces: Volume 2, Images Publishing Group, Melbourne, Australia, 2003

International Architectural Yearbook: No.2, Images Publishing Group, Melbourne, Australia, 1996

Interior Spaces of the USA: Volume 3, Images Publishing Group, Melbourne, Australia, 1997

Modern Wooden Houses, Process Architecture No. 18, Tokyo

Residential Spaces of the World: Volume 1, Images Publishing Group, Melbourne, Australia, 1994

Residential Spaces of the World: Volume 2, Images Publishing Group, Melbourne, Australia, 1997

Sardar, Zahid, *San Francisco Modern: Interiors, Architecture & Design*, Chronicle Books, San Francisco, 1998

Trulove, James Grason, *The New American House 4: Innovations in Residential Design and Construction*, Whitney Library of Design, Watson-Guptil Publications, New York, 2003

Periodicals

'1983 Design Awards', *Architectural Record*, July 1983

'Adding High Light', *Sunset*, January 1991, pp. 58–62

Anderson, Judith, 'The Architecture of Interior Design', *San Jose Mercury News*, April 3, 1988, pp. 20–26

Bertleson, Ann, 'Light Box', *Sunset Magazine*, October 1997, p. 118

Bertleson, Ann, 'Special Weapons and Tactics', *Northern California Home & Garden*, May 1990, pp. 44–51

Bertleson, Ann, 'Stairways', *Northern California Home & Garden*, October 1992, pp. 69,120

Botello, Alfredo, 'The Idea House', *Diablo Magazine*, March 1999, pp. 38–55

Brown-Martin, Darcy, 'The Mod Squad', *Diablo Magazine*, April 2002, pp. 48–51

'California Contextualism', *Architectural Record*, October 1983

Carlston, Lon M., 'Enough of the Earthtones', *Oakland Tribune*, August 15, 1976

Clark, Susannah, 'Comfort and Joy', *Diablo Magazine*, December 1994, pp. 36–38

Coupland, Ken, 'Bold Designs Forged From Fire', *San Francisco Examiner*, February 28, 1993, p. F-1

Dorn, Suzanne, 'Life Care Village Will Rise in Contra Costa', *Hospitality Design*, January–February 1993, p. 16

Eng, Rick, 'Permanent Fashion', *Designers West*, November 1991, pp. 80–83

Feldman, Deborah, 'Ironic Ionic', *Domus*, August 1980

'First AIA Honor Awards for Interiors', *Progressive Architecture*, June 1994, p. 70

Fuhrman, Janice, 'An Expansive Contemporary', *California Homes*, March–April 2002, pp. 82–89

Gold Award For Historic Preservation', *San Francisco Focus*, July 1993

Goode, Stephen, 'Chairs Do More Than Sit Outdoors', *Insight*, July 4, 1988

Gregory, Daniel, 'Checkerboards of Glass', *Sunset*, February 1982

Gregory, Daniel, 'Over The Garage and Across the Living Room – A Bright New Balcony Deck', *Sunset*, January 1982

Grossman, Daniel, 'Neo-Classical (Again)', *Harpers & Queen*, December 1980

Gundrum, Daniel, 'Utilitarian Chairs Gone Wild and Witty are Abloom in Cooper-Hewitt's Garden', *The New York Times*, May 19, 1988

Igonda, Marcelo, 'Tradicion Y Modernismo en Oakland, California', *La Opinion*, June 1983, pp. 12–13

Kinzie, Pam, 'Oakland/Berkeley Rebuild After 1991 Firestorm that Destroyed 2,800 Houses', *Architectural Record*, April 1993, p. 23

'Long-term Care Facility', *Progressive Architecture*, August 1993, p. 27

MacIsaac, Heather Smith, 'Ashes To Architecture', *House & Garden*, March 1993, p. 84

Mack, Mark, 'Small Spaces – Urban and Suburban Refinements', Fall 1980

MacMasters, Dan, 'A Bold Composition of Simple Forms', *Los Angeles Times Home Magazine*, March 5, 1978, pp. 14–15

Matteucci, Jeannie, 'The Devil Is In The Details', *San Francisco Chronicle*, October 15, 2003, pp. F-1, 6

Meckel, David, 'Exhibit On Post Fire Houses In The Oakland Hills', *Progressive Architecture*, March 1993, p. 22

Milshtein, Amy, 'Fitting Rooms', *Contract Design*, June 1994, pp. 70–73

Mitchem, Scott, 'Level Success', *Wallpaper*, October 2001, pp. 199–200

Mumford, Steve, 'The Icehouse', *Buildings*, June 1993, pp. 44–48

Nash, Kay Chabot, 'Kitchen Debates', *Diablo Magazine*, September 1999, pp. 46–47

O'hkura, Peggy, 'Uniquely Designed Building Taking Shape on Buchanan Mall', *Hokubei Mainichi*, April 9, 1982

Patel, Nina, 'Steel Away', *Remodeling*, September 2002, p. 58

'Rebirth of the Oakland Hills', *Sunset*, September 1994

'Rural Home Seems to Sprout From the Landscape', *California Builder*, February–March 1991, p. 16

Sakamoto, Timothy, 'Planet Architecture: Bay Area Modern', *In-D Digital*, 2000

Sardar, Zahid, 'Light Meter: Robert Swatt Illuminates Dramatic Spaces in Palo Alto', *Western Interiors and Design*, September–October 2003, pp. 74–83

Sardar, Zahid, 'Plane Thinking', *San Francisco Examiner Magazine*, May 17, 1998, pp. 76–79

Sardar, Zahid, 'Power Play', *San Francisco Examiner Magazine*, September 17, 2000, pp. 14–19

Smaus, Robert, 'They Reached for the View', *Los Angeles Times Home Magazine*, November, 1979

'Swatt & Stein', *Architectura*, Madrid, No. 220, September–October 1979, p. 36

'Swatt Architects Icehouse Project', *Hinge*, Volume 2, August 1994, pp. 36–37

Tucker, John G., 'Runway Visibility', *Interior Design*, April 1984

Wagner, Michael, 'California Casual', *Interiors*, January 1994, pp. 80–81

Acknowledgments, Drawing & Photography Credits

The projects in this book are the result of our collaboration with wonderful and dedicated clients who have trusted and shared our vision of modern architecture that is truly livable. Each project has benefited from the contributions of many talented people, most importantly my long-time partner Steven Stept, and associates David Burton and Matthew Mosey. Finally, I would like to thank my life-partner and superb critic, Cristina, for her special insights and many contributions to this work.

Robert Swatt

Drawing Credits

David Burton: 107 (ob)

Environmental Vision, Jeanie Fan: 107 (ot)

Jeanie Fan: 116 (o)

Kasia Kowalska-Ekstrand: 80 (or); 85 (ot, ob)

Robert Swatt: 20 (bl); 30 (a); 34 (br); 53 (br); 60 (a); 95 (t, a); 101 (a); 103 (b); 104 (bmb, tr); 110 (r); 112 (ot); 113 (b); 114 (r)

Photography Credits

Russell Abraham: back cover 2 (Swatt House); 9 (Fig 4 – Goldman Vacation House); 13 (Fig 12 – Carico House); 16, 22, 23 (t), 24, 26 (t, b) (Swatt House); 57, 58, 59 (t) (Greason House); 64 (tl, bl) (Woodland House); 99, 100 (ot), 101 (r) (Mayol House); 103 (tl, tr) (Shimmon House I); 106 (a) (GreenCity Lofts)

Charles Ansell: 11 (Fig 7 – Amito II)

Architecture and Design Collection, University Art Museum, University of California, Santa Barbara: 8 (Fig 2 – Nobby Knit Shop); 11 (Fig 9 – Wolfe House)

Richard Barnes: 34 (t, bl), 35, 37–41 (Kohavi House)

Jeanie Fan: 117 (l) (Tea Houses)

Joshua Freiwald: 10 (Fig 6 – Amito I)

Shelly Kappe: 7 (Robert Swatt and Ray Kappe)

Chas McGrath: 80 (ol), 81, 82 (l), 83, 84 (l, r), 86, 87 (l, a), 88 (bg, o), 89 (l, r), 90–91 (The Icehouse)

J.D. Peterson: 25 (l, r), 29 (Swatt House); 93–94, 95 (l) (Free Speech Movement Café)

Cesar Rubio: front cover (Palo Alto House); back cover 1 (Robert Swatt); 2 (Greason House); 13 (Fig 13 – Model of Swatt House); 18, 19 (tr, br), 20 (tl), 21, 27, 28 (t) (Swatt House); 36 (ml, bl) (Kohavi House); 42 (l), 43–44, 45 (t, b), 46 (ol), 48 (t, b), 49–52, 53 (tl, tr), 54 (t), 55 (Palo Alto House); 56, 59 (b) (Greason House); 61–62, 63 (l, a), 65–66, 67 (tl, tr, bl), 68, 69 (tl, r, bl) (Woodland House); 70, 72 (t, b), 73, 74 (tl), 75–76, 77 (l, r), 78 (a, l), 79 (Conrad House); 92 (r), 96, 97 (bg, b) (Free Speech Movement Café); 111 (ot), 112 (ob) (Morley House); 115 (otl, otr), 117 (tr) (Tea Houses)

Mark Schwartz: 31–33 (Kohavi House)

Julius Shulman: 8 (Fig 1 – Emerson Junior High); 9 (Fig 3 – Kappe House); 10 (Fig 5 – Drake House); 12 (Fig 10 – Lovell House)

Robert Swatt: 11 (Fig 8 – Foster/Feldman House); 12 (Fig 11 – a drawing of Sommers House); 104 (tl, ml), 105 (or) (Shimmon House I)

Abbreviations

Above (a), Background (bg), Bottom (b), Bottom left (bl), Bottom middle & bottom (bmb), Bottom right (br), Left (l), Middle left (ml), Middle left (ml), Opposite (o), Opposite bottom (ob), Opposite left (ol), Opposite right (or), Opposite top (ot), Opposite top left (otl), Opposite top right (otr), Right (r), Top (t), Top right (tr)

Index

Every effort has been made to trace the original
source of copyright material contained in this book.
The publishers would be pleased to hear from
copyright holders to rectify any error or omissions.
The information and illustrations in this publication
have been prepared and supplied by Swatt Architects.
While all reasonable efforts have been made to
ensure accuracy, the publishers do not, under any
circumstances, accept responsibility for errors,
omissions and representations express or implied.